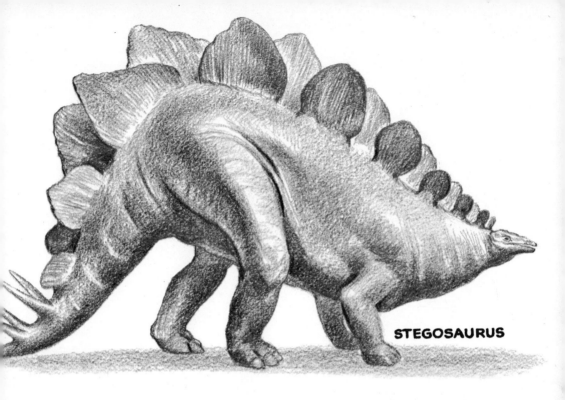

STEGOSAURUS

DINOSAURS

by **HERBERT S. ZIM**

illustrated by James Gordon Irving

WILLIAM MORROW & COMPANY   1954

Grateful recognition is given by the author to Dr. Bryan Patterson of the Chicago Museum of Natural History, Chicago, Illinois, for reading and criticizing the manuscript.

The artist wishes to express his gratitude to the American Museum of Natural History for making available its series of dinosaur models by W.P.A. workers and others. Many of the illustrations have been based on them.

See Page 64 for pronunciation of the dinosaurs' names.

Library of Congress Catalog Card No. 54-5080.

26   27   28   82   81   80

BRONTOSAURUS

Every day hundreds of people stop and stare at the great dinosaur skeletons in museums. Even with the huge bones in front of them, they find it hard to believe that such creatures once lived. There is no doubt that these great reptiles did live. This is an astonishing fact, since no man has ever seen them alive.

3

MILLIONS OF YEARS

0
10 AGE OF MAMMALS
70 MILLION YEARS

100 AGE OF REPTILES
120 MILLION YEARS

200 AGE OF
ANCIENT LIFE
350 MILLION YEARS

300 AMPHIBIANS

FISH

400

INVERTEBRATES

500

0
1
2
3
4
5
6
7
8
9
10

AGE
OF
MAN

Dinosaurs were common everyday animals for a period of some 100 million years. About 75 million years ago the whole group began to die out, and all were gone millions of years before the first men lived. Dinosaurs lived during the Mesozoic era, or the Age of Reptiles, a period which lasted about 120 million years. Many kinds of flying, running, crawling, and swimming reptiles lived during this time, but none were as exciting as the dinosaurs.

To think of dinosaurs only as huge earth-shaking beasts is a mistake. Some dinosaurs were the largest animals ever to live on land, but many other kinds were small. The smallest were no larger than chickens or dogs. Some plodded along slowly, clumsy and heavy-footed. Others were fleet as rabbits. Many browsed on grasses and soft marsh plants. A smaller number of flesh eaters fought with and devoured their weaker companions.

We shall probably never know how many kinds of dinosaurs there were. The marvel is that we know anything about them at all.

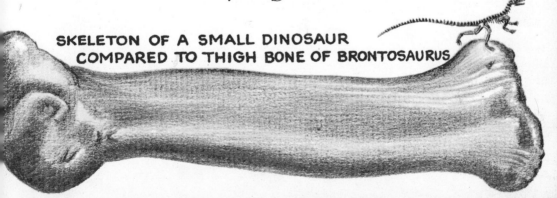

SKELETON OF A SMALL DINOSAUR
COMPARED TO THIGH BONE OF BRONTOSAURUS

Their story has been pieced together from bones, teeth, and other fossils dug out of the rocks in out-of-the-way places. Remains of many different kinds of dinosaurs have already been discovered. No doubt a great many more dinosaurs than we have found flourished during the Age of Reptiles.

FOSSILS BURIED IN LAYERS OF SEDIMENTARY ROCK

MAN

PTERODACTYL

FOSSIL FISH

TRILOBITE

FOSSILS

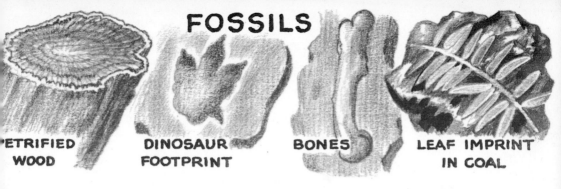

PETRIFIED WOOD   DINOSAUR FOOTPRINT   BONES   LEAF IMPRINT IN COAL

Scientists read the story of ancient life from fossils in the same way that a detective pieces clues together to solve a mystery. Fossil clues to dinosaurs and other kinds of ancient animals are not easily found. Fossils are formed when a plant or animal is buried under sand or mud, or under ashes from a volcano. This preserves the remains and, if conditions are right, a fossil may form.

Sometimes water containing minerals such as lime and silica seeps through the mud or sand. The minerals slowly replace the hard parts of the plant or animal. Bones, teeth, shells, and occasionally softer parts like skin, are partly or completely replaced by minerals.

7

This may be done in such detail that every tiny part is preserved in exactly its original shape and form. Petrified wood and petrified bone are made in this way.

Fossils form in other ways, too. Sometimes only the imprint of a shell or the footprint of a dinosaur remains as mud hardens. This makes a *mold,* another form of fossil. The mold may later fill with mud or sand which hardens into a *cast,* making an exact copy of a shell, bone, footprint, or even a whole animal or plant.

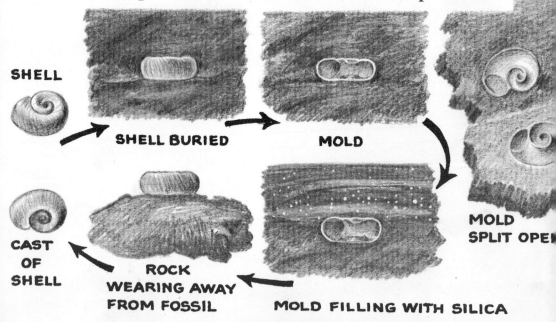

SHELL

SHELL BURIED

MOLD

MOLD SPLIT OPEN

CAST OF SHELL

ROCK WEARING AWAY FROM FOSSIL

MOLD FILLING WITH SILICA

Fossils of dinosaurs are hard to find. Land animals do not get buried under preserving layers of sand and mud as often as shellfish and other water animals do. Besides, rocks which are old enough to contain fossils of dinosaurs may be buried deep under layers of newer rocks. Where these rocks do come to the surface, there is only a small chance that fossils will be exposed in them. It takes patience, skill, and luck to find fossil dinosaur bones.

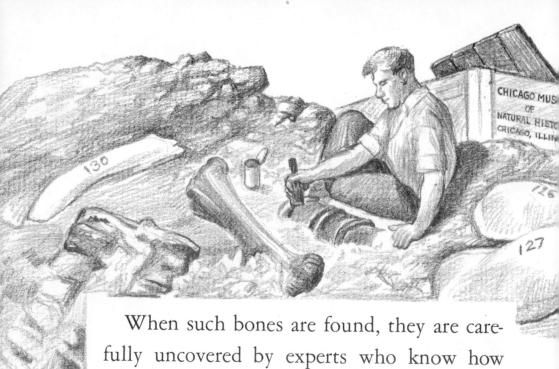

When such bones are found, they are carefully uncovered by experts who know how fragile fossil bone can be. Then the bones and the rock close to them are covered with plaster and burlap for protection. They are carefully removed, packed, and shipped to one of the great museums or universities. Here the bones are cleaned, studied, and mounted. The experts compare them with other fossil bones and with the bones of living animals. Each detail is important. A lump on a bone may show

where muscles were attached. The form of teeth tells whether the dinosaur was a plant eater or a flesh eater. The expert must start with a thorough knowledge of living animals. Using this knowledge as a guide, he may build from the bones he has found a complete skeleton of the dinosaur, or even a model as it may have looked when it was alive.

Our knowledge of the dinosaurs is based on their bones. From the bones it is possible to tell their size, and also something of their appearance and habits. Bones also show how the various kinds of dinosaurs were related to one another. Fossils in older rocks tell some of the story of where dinosaurs came from, who their ancestors were, and how different kinds developed.

Dinosaurs were reptiles, and all reptiles are backboned animals. Dinosaurs can be traced from ancestor to ancestor back to the first backboned animals—small, fishlike creatures that lived in streams and brooks and probably developed backbones about 350 million years

CHEIROLEPIS

OSTEOLEPIS

EARLY KINDS OF FISH

AMONG THE FIRST BACKBONED ANIMALS

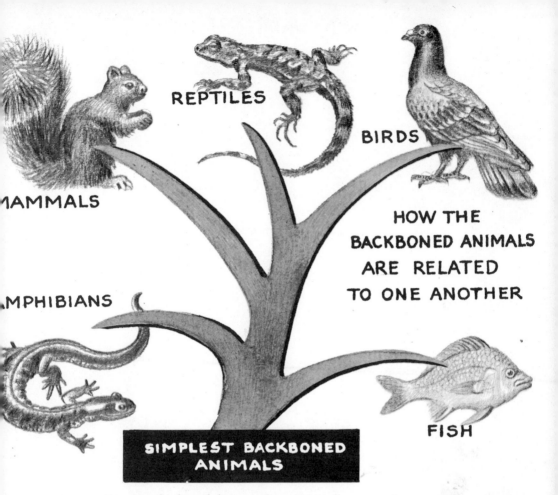

REPTILES

BIRDS

MAMMALS

HOW THE
BACKBONED ANIMALS
ARE RELATED
TO ONE ANOTHER

AMPHIBIANS

FISH

SIMPLEST BACKBONED
ANIMALS

ago. It took backboned animals another 100 million years to develop limbs for crawling and lungs for breathing, so they could first venture out on the land. This step paved the way for the many kinds of land animals that soon became more and more common.

MODERN AMPHIBIANS

FROG

TOAD

SALAMANDER

The first backboned land animals were the amphibians. Amphibians we see today are frogs, toads, and salamanders. Most of the early amphibians were small. A few grew as large as or larger than alligators. Most were clumsy swamp creatures which fed on insects and other small animals. One group of amphibians became the ancestors of the reptiles.

ANCIENT AMPHIBIANS
ABOUT 250 MILLION YEARS AGO

ERYOPS

DIPLOCAULUS

SOME COLD-BLOODED ANIMALS

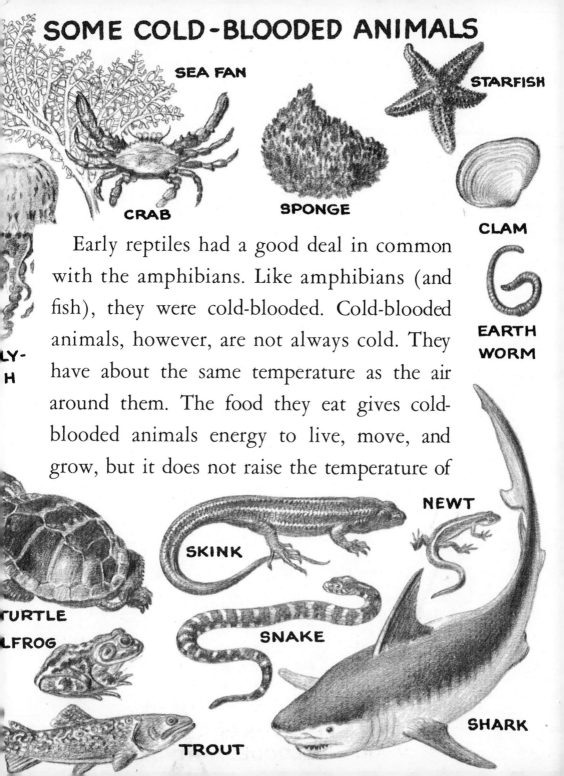

SEA FAN

STARFISH

CRAB

SPONGE

CLAM

EARTH WORM

LY-H

Early reptiles had a good deal in common with the amphibians. Like amphibians (and fish), they were cold-blooded. Cold-blooded animals, however, are not always cold. They have about the same temperature as the air around them. The food they eat gives cold-blooded animals energy to live, move, and grow, but it does not raise the temperature of

NEWT

SKINK

TURTLE

LFROG

SNAKE

SHARK

TROUT

their bodies more than a degree or so. The food eaten by warm-blooded animals helps keep their bodies at a fixed temperature—usually a good deal warmer than the air. Your body temperature is a bit over 98 degrees; a dog's is 102 degrees and a chicken's 101 degrees.

BAT
104°

MAN
98.6°

DOG
102°

COW
101°

CAT
101.6°

101°
CHICKEN

TEMPERATURES OF WARM - BLOODED ANIMALS

The temperature of cold-blooded reptiles varies with the day. On a hot day, a reptile may be even warmer than a warm-blooded bird. On a cold day, reptiles may be so sluggish that they cannot move fast enough to get food or escape their enemies.

On the other hand, most of the earliest reptiles showed themselves more highly developed than amphibians in three different ways. First, their skeleton was better built for strength and support. Reptiles could run faster than amphibians. The second difference was their skin. Amphibians often have smooth, moist skins. Reptiles developed skin with scales, plates, and later with bony armor. This meant protection against sun, dryness, disease, and enemies.

17

AMPHIBIANS

REPTILES

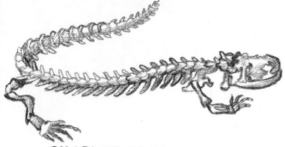

SIMPLER SKELETON
SLOW-MOVING   POOR SUPPORT

MORE ADVANCED SKELETON
BETTER SUPPORT   FASTER

SKIN MOIST, THIN
LITTLE PROTECTION

SKIN SCALY OR WITH PLATES
PROTECTION AGAINST DRYING

EGGS - NOT PROTECTED
NO SHELL, LITTLE STORED FOOD

EGG - LEATHERY SHELL
MORE FOOD, MEMBRANES FOR
BREATHING

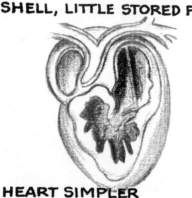

HEART SIMPLER
POORER PUMP

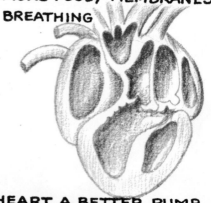

HEART A BETTER PUMP

The third and most important advance the reptiles made was in the type of egg they laid. Fish and amphibians lay small jelly-like eggs in water. Even the few amphibians which can live away from water must return to pond, stream, or swamp to lay their eggs.

Reptile eggs, unlike those of amphibians, have a hard or horny covering. Inside the egg is a yolk with a reserve supply of food and a membrane to protect the young reptile and enable it to breathe while still within the shell.

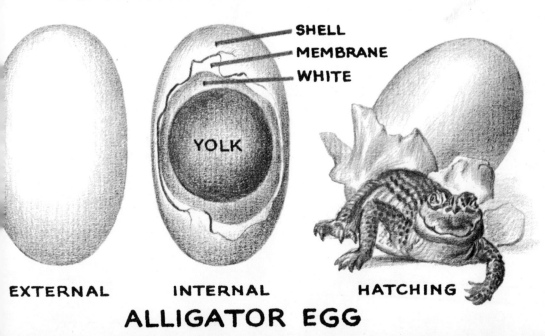

SHELL
MEMBRANE
WHITE
YOLK

EXTERNAL   INTERNAL   HATCHING
ALLIGATOR EGG

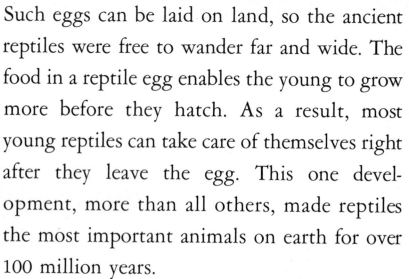

Such eggs can be laid on land, so the ancient reptiles were free to wander far and wide. The food in a reptile egg enables the young to grow more before they hatch. As a result, most young reptiles can take care of themselves right after they leave the egg. This one development, more than all others, made reptiles the most important animals on earth for over 100 million years.

STYRACOSAURUS

Of all the early reptiles, the cotylosaurs were the most common. Most were small or medium-sized, four-legged, crawling reptiles which looked something like clumsy over-grown lizards. Many different kinds of cotylosaurs developed, but all became extinct before the Age of Reptiles was one quarter over. It was from these reptiles, with skulls very much like the old amphibians, that all other groups of reptiles developed—the dinosaurs, the great flying and swimming reptiles, and those that still live today: the turtles, lizards, snakes, and

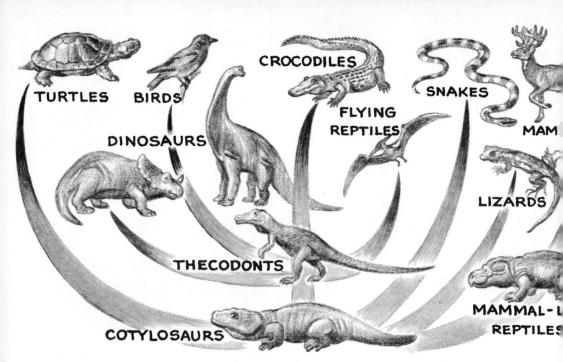

TURTLES BIRDS

DINOSAURS

CROCODILES

FLYING REPTILES

SNAKES

MAM

LIZARDS

THECODONTS

MAMMAL-L REPTILES

COTYLOSAURS

crocodiles. Even birds and mammals can be traced back, through group after group, to their ancient ancestors—the cotylosaurs.

The cotylosaurs might be considered grand-fathers of all the reptiles. Their descendants, the thecodonts that lived about 200 million years ago, were the dinosaurs' direct ancestors. Thecodonts were active reptiles. The skeletons show they had a more advanced kind of skull than cotylosaurs. They clearly prove that several kinds ran on their hind legs. Compare the picture of your hip bones with those of a four-legged animal. While both have the same bones, notice the differences in how they are formed. The hip bones of reptiles are different from ours, but these bones show that some thecodonts walked on their hind legs. The size of the front and hind leg bones bears this out.

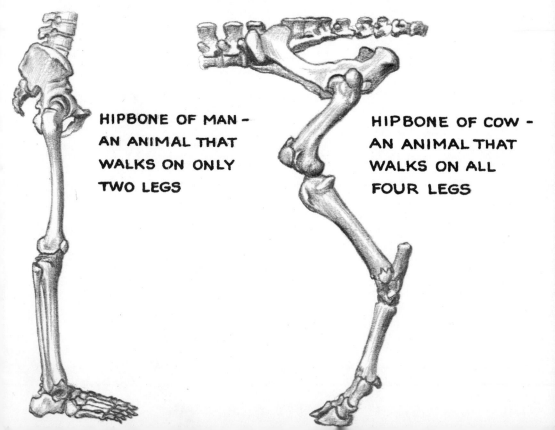

HIPBONE OF MAN –
AN ANIMAL THAT
WALKS ON ONLY
TWO LEGS

HIPBONE OF COW –
AN ANIMAL THAT
WALKS ON ALL
FOUR LEGS

By the time the thecodonts had developed, other groups of reptiles had branched off. One of these groups gave rise to the mammals. Another developed into present-day turtles. The thecodonts, in addition to being ancestors of all the dinosaurs, were also ancestors of such different animals as crocodiles, birds, and pterosaurs—the only reptiles that ever learned to fly. It is through this long path leading from one group of animals to another, and moving slowly forward for millions upon millions of years, that we finally reach the dinosaurs.

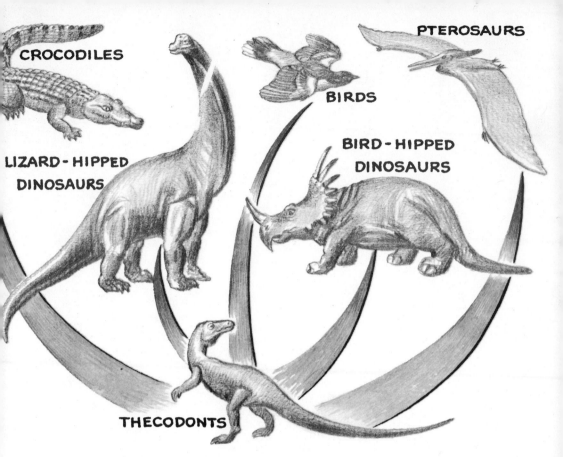

CROCODILES

PTEROSAURS

BIRDS

LIZARD-HIPPED
DINOSAURS

BIRD-HIPPED
DINOSAURS

THECODONTS

Remember that all the dinosaurs did not live at the same time but over a period of about 100 million years. They did not all live in the same place, and distinct kinds have been found in each continent. Let's take a look at the different dinosaurs, especially at the largest and most famous of them.

BRACHIOSAURUS

Truly the world's largest land animal, brachiosaurus weighed about 50 tons—ten times as much as an elephant. The front legs of this swamp and river dweller were longer than the hind legs. It fed on plants.

STEGOSAURUS

The oddly armored stegosaurs, 20 feet long, were taller in the middle than at either end. Four long, sharp spikes on their tails served to protect them from their enemies. They browsed on small plants.

ORNITHOLESTES (LEFT)

This small, 6-foot-tall dinosaur was light, fast, and almost birdlike as it hunted birds and other small animals for food. Like some of its thecodont ancestors, ornitholestes ran on its hind legs.

ALLOSAURUS (RIGHT)

Allosaurs were heavier-built dinosaurs than ornitholestes. They reached a length of 35 feet. Stalking its prey, allosaurus walked on its heavy hind legs, using its tail for balancing.

BRONTOSAURUS

Brontosaurus was one of the largest land animals. At least 70 feet long, it weighed some 35 tons. A swamp dweller, it fed on water plants—by the ton. This four-legged giant came from two-legged ancestors.

DIPLODOCUS

The high-placed nostrils show that this plant eater liked to lie safe and hidden in water with only the top of its head showing. Diplodocus was longer than brontosaurus. One skeleton measures 87 feet.

PROTOCERATOPS

Fossils of this ancestor of triceratops were found in the Mongolian Desert of Asia. Many skeletons—from newborn to adults—were unearthed, as well as nests of eggs, some containing unhatched young.

TRICERATOPS

Triceratops and their kin were fierce, horned dinosaurs with spreading skull bones, which protected the entire front of the body. They developed hooked beaks for tearing loose the plants on which they fed.

TYRANNOSAURUS (LEFT)

This "king of dinosaurs" developed much later than allo-saurus. Tyrannosaurus preyed on the large, plant-eating swamp dinosaurs. It grew 50 feet long, towered 20 feet high, and weighed perhaps 10 tons.

ANKYLOSAURUS (RIGHT)

As stegosaurs died out, the ankylosaurs became more com-mon. About 10 feet long, they were armored with overlap-ping bony plates and clublike tails. They moved slowly, like living tanks, feeding on plants.

ANATOSAURS (LEFT)

Anatosaurs were duck-billed swamp dinosaurs. They and their kin walked on large hind legs, grazing on grasses and tender shoots. Their 3-toed footprints are found in rocks formed from swamp mud.

IGUANODON (RIGHT). LENGTH 30 FT.

In 1822, a British doctor's wife found strange teeth in rocks near her home. Research showed they came from a giant reptile, like the iguana lizard, and so this dinosaur was named iguanodon.

These are just a few of the dinosaurs, a famous group of reptiles which turned out not to be a single group of reptiles at all. Dinosaur bones, teeth, and footprints had been known for some 25 years before the name *dinosaur* was applied to these extinct reptiles, over 100 years ago. Much later, after many more fossils were discovered and studied, it became clear to the experts that the dinosaurs were not one group of reptiles but two. Two

DINOSAUR FOOTPRINTS WERE ONCE THOUGHT MADE BY GIGANTIC BIRDS

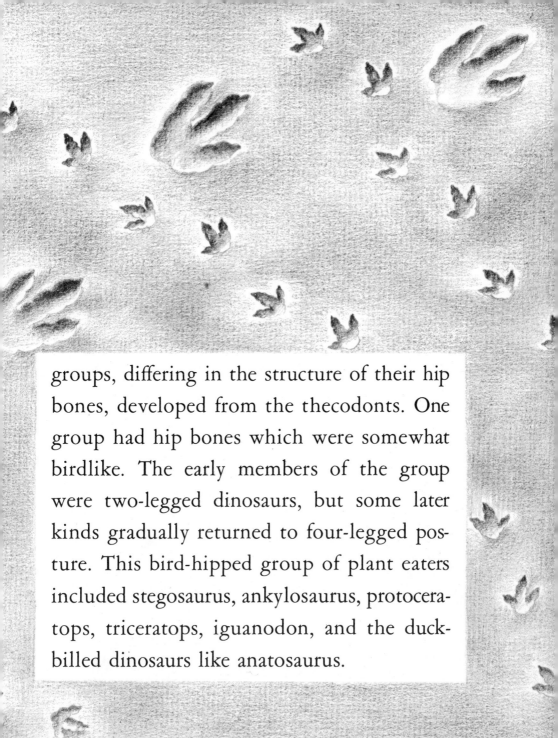

groups, differing in the structure of their hip bones, developed from the thecodonts. One group had hip bones which were somewhat birdlike. The early members of the group were two-legged dinosaurs, but some later kinds gradually returned to four-legged posture. This bird-hipped group of plant eaters included stegosaurus, ankylosaurus, protoceratops, triceratops, iguanodon, and the duck-billed dinosaurs like anatosaurus.

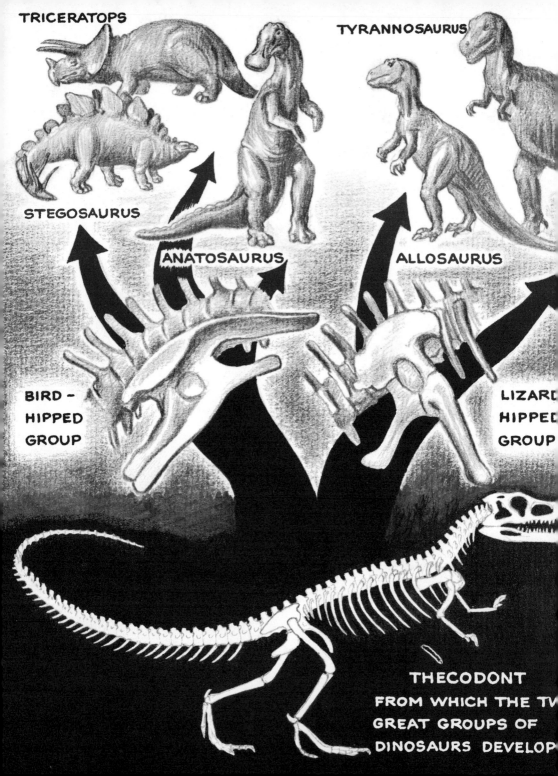

The other group, with lizardlike hip bones, also started as two-legged dinosaurs. But they developed in two ways. One produced the giant swamp dinosaurs: brontosaurus, diplodocus, and brachiosaurus. The other gave us the large, two-legged flesh eaters: allosaurus, tyrannosaurus, and their kin.

One of the strangest facts in the story of dinosaurs is that certain kinds which looked similar actually belonged to different groups. They developed by different routes from their common thecodont ancestors. Careful study of fossil bones has revealed the unusual story of these very different dinosaurs that looked so much alike.

TWO-LEGGED LIZARD-HIPPED DINOSAUR

TWO-LEGGED BIRD-HIPPED DINOSAUR

TYRANNOSAURUS

DUCK-BILL

During the Age of Reptiles, thousands upon thousands of generations of dinosaurs were born and died. With each nest of eggs that hatched, there was a new chance for those that were somewhat different—or better adapted to live—to grow up, spread out, and raise their young. Sometimes these newer forms survived while others died off, so that as the millions of years passed, the dinosaurs spread and changed.

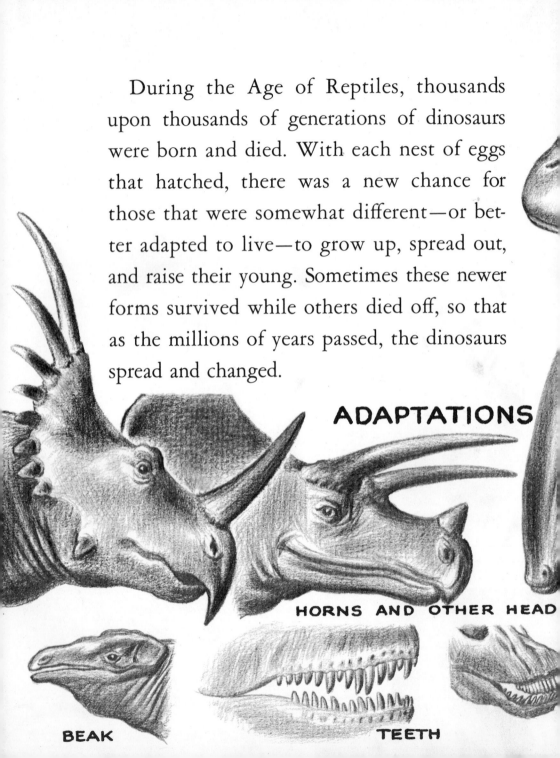

ADAPTATIONS

HORNS AND OTHER HEAD

BEAK

TEETH

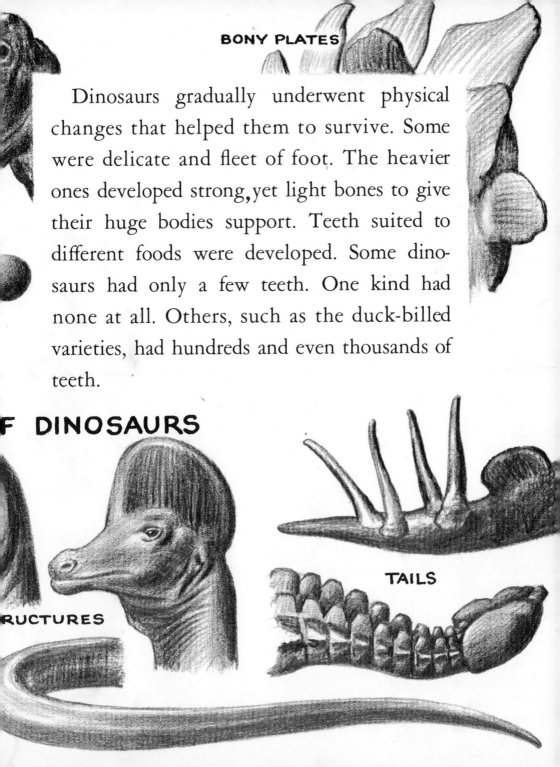

BONY PLATES

Dinosaurs gradually underwent physical changes that helped them to survive. Some were delicate and fleet of foot. The heavier ones developed strong, yet light bones to give their huge bodies support. Teeth suited to different foods were developed. Some dinosaurs had only a few teeth. One kind had none at all. Others, such as the duck-billed varieties, had hundreds and even thousands of teeth.

F DINOSAURS

RUCTURES

TAILS

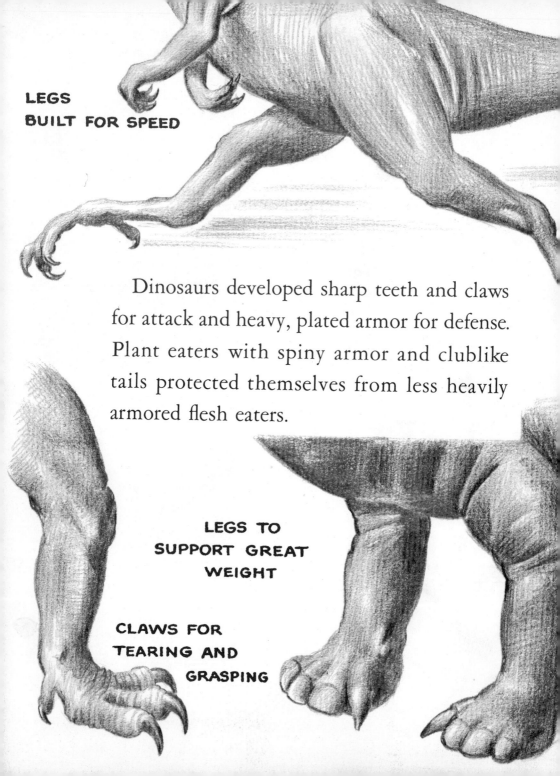

LEGS BUILT FOR SPEED

Dinosaurs developed sharp teeth and claws for attack and heavy, plated armor for defense. Plant eaters with spiny armor and clublike tails protected themselves from less heavily armored flesh eaters.

LEGS TO SUPPORT GREAT WEIGHT

CLAWS FOR TEARING AND GRASPING

Speed was the protection of smaller dinosaurs. One small kind developed a thick skull with solid bone nearly a foot thick. This hardly seems worth while; it had so little brain to protect!

The climate over most of the earth was mild or warm during the long Age of Reptiles. This gave cold-blooded animals a chance to spread into areas where they could not live today. Many regions were moist as well as warm and plants were plentiful.

A warm climate was truly the lifeblood of the great reptiles. It made possible huge supplies of plant and animal food. Giant ferns and other soft plants grew in profusion in the

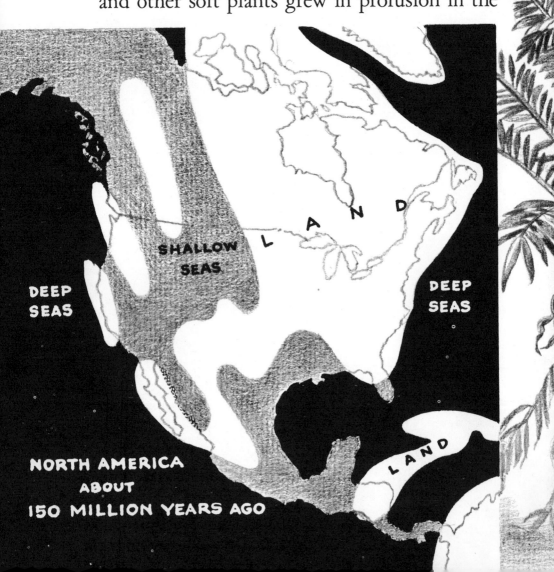

DEEP SEAS

SHALLOW SEAS

L A N D

DEEP SEAS

LAND

NORTH AMERICA
ABOUT
150 MILLION YEARS AGO

moist lowlands. Even the drier regions were far from barren. Cycads and palmlike trees were common, and broad-leaved trees such as magnolias and maples began to appear toward the end of the era.

CYCAD

COMMON PLANTS OF THE AGE OF REP- TILES. SOME STILL LIVE TODAY THOUGH THEY ARE NO LONGER COMMON.

GINKGO OR MAIDENHAIR TREE

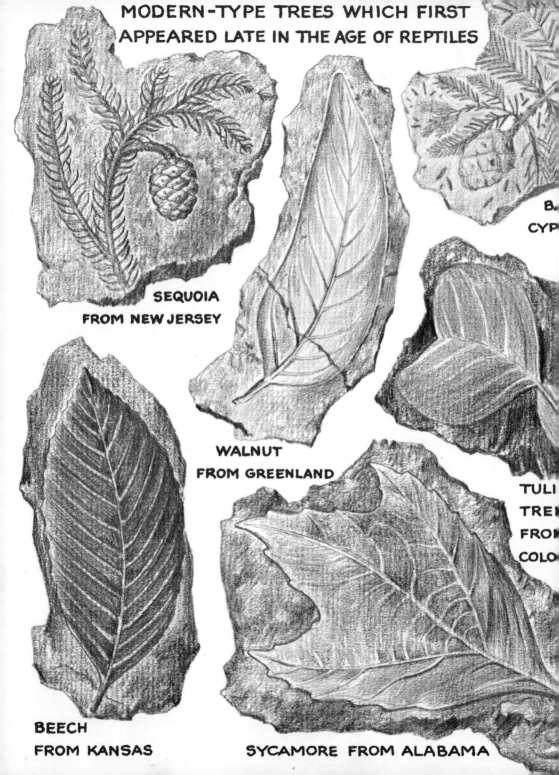

MODERN-TYPE TREES WHICH FIRST APPEARED LATE IN THE AGE OF REPTILES

SEQUOIA FROM NEW JERSEY

B.
CYP

WALNUT
FROM GREENLAND

TULI
TRE
FRO
COLO

BEECH
FROM KANSAS

SYCAMORE FROM ALABAMA

Climate favored the dinosaurs, but it was not the cause of their giant size. Every living thing has limits to its size. The average height for all the human race is 5 feet 5 inches, and very few groups of people average more than a few inches above or below this. When a person grows more than a foot above average, the growth may be due to overactivity of a

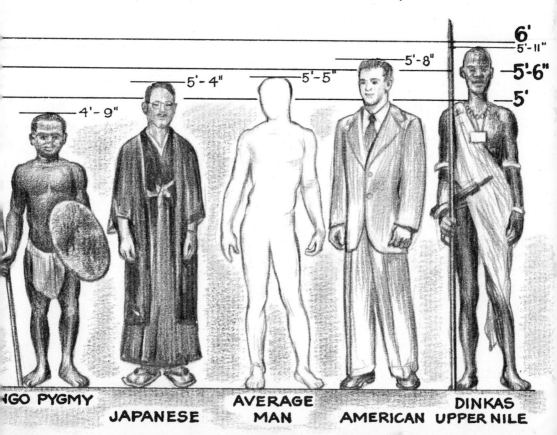

6'
5'-11"
5'-8"
5'-4"
5'-5"
5'-6"
4'-9"
5'

IGO PYGMY

JAPANESE

AVERAGE MAN

AMERICAN

DINKAS UPPER NILE

small but important gland in the brain. This is the pituitary gland, the source of a chemical which makes animals grow. An overactive pituitary gland makes giants; an underactive one makes dwarfs.

GIANT - OVERACTIVE
PITUITARY GLAND
HEIGHT - 7' 9"

NORMAL - HEIGHT - 5' 10

DWARF - UNDERAC
PITUITARY GLA
HEIGHT - 4'

The study of the skull bones of dinosaurs shows more than the shape and form of the head. It may also show the shape and size of the space occupied by the brain. Since the pituitary gland is at the base of the brain, an expert can sometimes estimate its size from the pattern of the skull bones. In the case of the giant dinosaurs, the pituitary was found to be unusually large compared to the size of the rest of the brain. This may have caused these dinosaurs to grow to giant size, but there is no way of being certain, since fossil bones are all we have to go by.

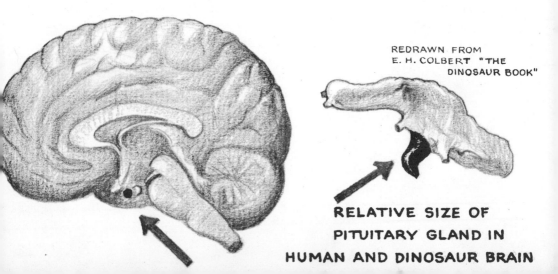

REDRAWN FROM
E. H. COLBERT "THE
DINOSAUR BOOK"

RELATIVE SIZE OF PITUITARY GLAND IN HUMAN AND DINOSAUR BRAIN

Even the chemicals from the pituitary gland cannot make any kind of animal continue to grow larger and larger. If giant animals are to survive, they must develop changes in skeleton and body to support their weight and enable them to get enough food. The great dinosaurs probably came as close to these limits as any land animal could get; but water animals, supported by the buoyancy

BLUE WHALE
90 - 100 FEET LONG
WEIGHT 120 - 150 TONS

BRACHIOSAURUS
75 FEET LONG   WEIGHT ABOUT 50 TONS

of the sea, have grown much larger. The
blue whales grow 90 to 100 feet long and
weigh from 120 to 150 tons. They are longer
than the largest dinosaur and nearly three
times as heavy.

DIAN ELEPHANT
FEET HIGH
EIGHT ABOUT 5 TONS

While part of the dinosaur's brain accounts for its great size, the rest of its brain is nothing to get excited about. Compared to animals we know today, the dinosaurs were very stupid. They could never have learned to do tricks, like circus animals, and would never have made good pets. Compared to the size of their bodies, their brains were unusually

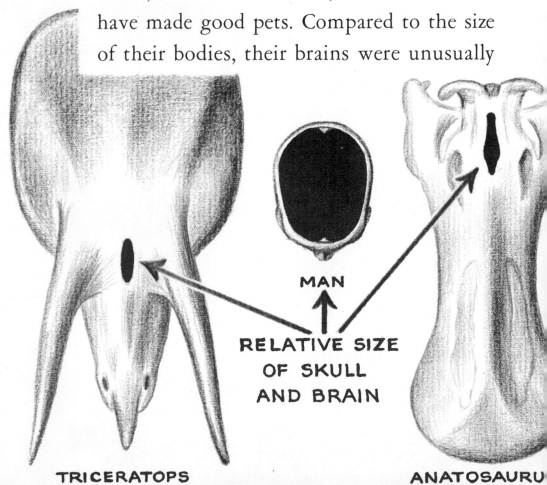

MAN

RELATIVE SIZE
OF SKULL
AND BRAIN

TRICERATOPS

ANATOSAURU

small. The weight of your body is about 50 times that of your brain. A dog weighs 170 times its brain weight, a horse 700, an elephant 1000, and a whale 7000 times. As near as we can guess, the figure for a dinosaur would be much higher—perhaps as high as 25,000 or 50,000. No one is too sure of the weight of dinosaurs or the weight of their brains, but dinosaurs were certainly less brainy than even the simplest mammals.

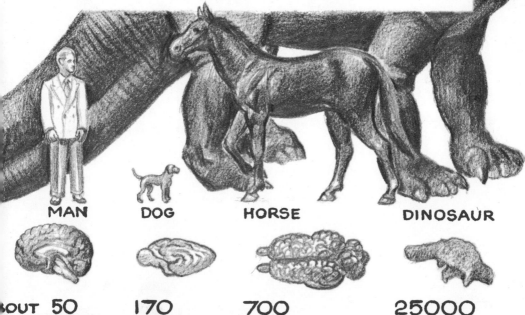

MAN   DOG   HORSE   DINOSAUR

ABOUT 50 TIMES   170 TIMES   700 TIMES   25000 TIMES

WEIGHT OF BODY COMPARED TO BRAIN

In spite of tall tales of dinosaurs still living in hidden tropical swamps, scientists believe they all died off millions of years ago. This did not happen overnight, but even before the Age of Reptiles ended, the heyday of the great dinosaurs had passed. There were probably many reasons for this. The climate, which had long favored reptiles, may have become slightly colder. New mountains were pushing up in several parts of the world, and a general rising of the land may have helped cause this change. As the land rose, the shallow seas and the swamps shrank in size. It was here that many of the great reptiles lived, feeding on the rich vegetation.

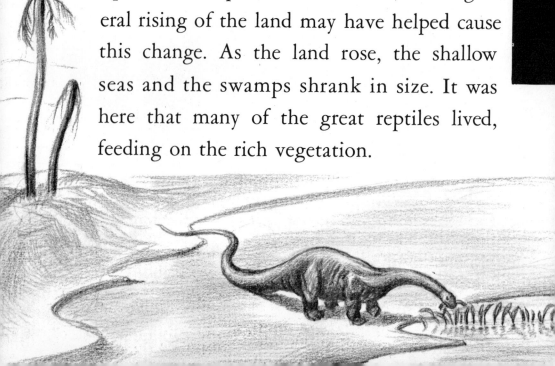

A SMALL PART OF THE ROCKY MOUNTAIN FRONT NEAR BOULDER, COLORADO WHERE FLAT LAYERS OF ROCK WERE FOLDED AND PUSHED UP

WHERE MOUNTAIN RANGES WERE SLOWLY PUSHED AND FOLDED UPWARD TOWARD THE END OF THE AGE OF REPTILES

Other reasons for their disappearance perhaps lay in the dinosaurs themselves. Some had become so large and overdeveloped that even when conditions were good it was hard for them to get enough food. With their lim-

A 35-TON BRONTOSAU[...]
MAY HAVE NEEDED ABOU[...]
1000 POUNDS OF FOOD DA[...]
COLD-BLOODED ANIMA[...]
USUALLY NEED LESS F[...]
THAN WARM-BLOO[...]
ANIMALS THE[...]
SAME SIZE

A 5-TON ELEPHANT
EATS 100-200 POUNDS
OF LEAVES AND PLANTS
DAILY

ited brain, they could not learn to change their ways. It is also possible that the large pituitary gland did more than make dinosaurs gigantic. It may have affected them in other ways that made it harder for them to survive.

Finally, new enemies of the dinosaurs came on the scene. They were not larger, stronger beasts. They were both smaller and weaker, but they were more intelligent. These were the mammals, which had developed from a different group of reptiles than the one that gave rise to the dinosaurs. Mammals are warm-blooded. Many are good hunters and are active at night. It is quite possible that these

small, brainy animals learned to feed on dinosaur eggs and thus destroyed many of the
young. As conditions for living grew worse,
this loss of young might have been an important factor in the dinosaurs' failure to sur-

vive. All these things, and no doubt others, made life more and more difficult for dinosaurs. The last of them died out about 75 million years ago. Only in the past century have we learned their story.

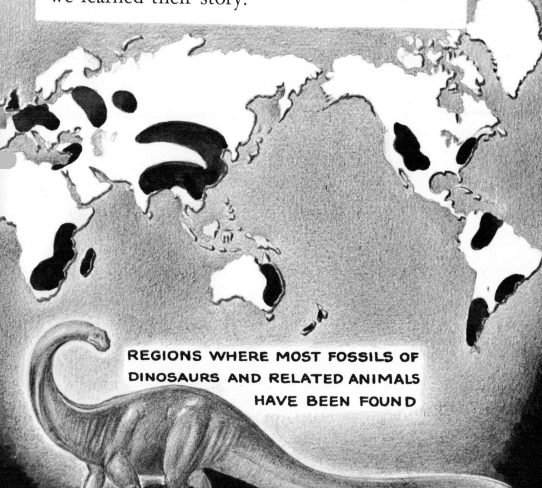

REGIONS WHERE MOST FOSSILS OF
DINOSAURS AND RELATED ANIMALS
HAVE BEEN FOUND

In all the animal world the dinosaurs had no equal. Neither has the wonderful story of how scientists, using clues from bones, teeth, footprints, and from the rocks themselves, have unraveled the dinosaurs' secret. In doing so, scientists have learned that size and strength are not the most important factors in the survival of an animal. Brains are more important. They provide the ability to change

60   50   40

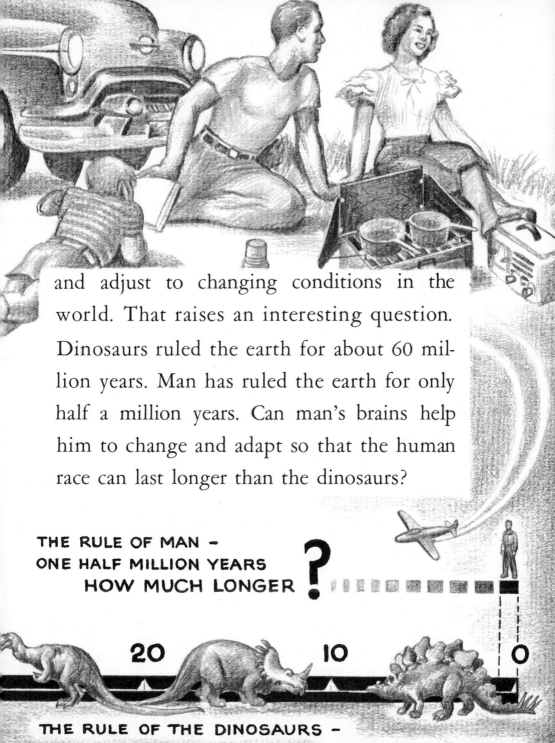

and adjust to changing conditions in the world. That raises an interesting question. Dinosaurs ruled the earth for about 60 million years. Man has ruled the earth for only half a million years. Can man's brains help him to change and adapt so that the human race can last longer than the dinosaurs?

THE RULE OF MAN —
ONE HALF MILLION YEARS
HOW MUCH LONGER ?

20   10   0

THE RULE OF THE DINOSAURS —
60 MILLION YEARS

Names of dinosaurs and other reptiles are not hard to say. They are pronounced very much as they are written. These names are Greek. Each syllable is sounded. The syllable in capital letters is accented. The ending *saur* or *saurus* means lizard; the ending *dont* means tooth.

Reptile	Pronounced
Allosaurus	al-lo-SAWR-us
Anatosaurus	an-at-o-SAWR-us
Ankylosaurus	an-kile-o-SAWR-us
Brachiosaurus	brak-e-o-SAWR-us
Brontosaurus	bront-o-SAWR-us
Cotylosaur	ko-tile-o-SAWR
Dinosaur	DINE-o-sawr
Diplodocus	dip-LAH-do-cus
Iguanodon	i-GWAN-o-don
Ornitholestes	orn-i-tho-LES-teez
Protoceratops	pro-toe-SER-a-tops
Stegosaurus	steg-o-SAWR-us
Thecodont	theek-o-DONT
Triceratops	try-SER-a-tops
Tyrannosaurus	tie-ran-o-SAWR-us